... lucky
... you
birthday in the
you — and so
lucky that you're
my dad. Happy
happy birthday!
love, Lis

Flowers at my Feet

THE WILD FLOWERS OF BRITAIN AND IRELAND IN PHOTOGRAPHS

Flowers at my Feet

THE WILD FLOWERS OF BRITAIN AND IRELAND IN PHOTOGRAPHS

PLANTLIFE

Bob Gibbons & David Woodfall

HarperCollins*Publishers*
77–85 Fulham Palace Road
London
W6 8JB

www.collins.co.uk

Collins is a registered trademark of
HarperCollins Publishers Ltd.

First published 2002

10 9 8 7 6 5 4 3 2

08 07 06 05 04 03

ISBN 0 00 220213 1

Designed by SMITH
Colour origination by Colourscan, Singapore
Printed and bound by The Bath Press

Endpaper photograph
**Rosebay Willow-herb and Meadowsweet,
North Wales**
Adjacent to a limestone quarry owned by
Tarmac Central Ltd, and a nature reserve Coed
y Felin, managed by the North Wales Wildlife
Trust. This tiny meadow appears to be given no
special consideration; like many such places it
retains its wildflower interest probably due to a
blocked drain and an occasionally flooding
adjacent river. It is a vivid illustration of the
vulnerability of many of our important wildflower
sites. (DW)

Title page photograph
Mullion Cove, The Lizard, Cornwall
Here the fabulous cliffs south of Mullion Cove
are covered with Sea Campion, Thrift, Kidney
Vetch and Bluebells; photograph taken at dawn
on a morning in early May. (BG)

CONTENTS

FOREWORD
Dr Jane Smart
Executive Director
Plantlife

People need plants and plants need people. It is a simple fact of life. Plants are fundamental to our daily lives: our food, our medicines, our clothes, our books, and our furniture. We can also look beyond to the life-sustaining carbon sinks of the world's great forests, or the wetlands that help prevent flooding and are the first line of resistance to rising sea-levels. When the plants go the animals, the birds and the insects go too. Plants sustain the quality of life we live, and we lose them at our peril.

The losses of plant species and habitats over the last 50 years have been devastating. On average, each county in the UK now loses one plant species every year. Coupled with climate change, the future for our native flora could be bleak. Enormous tracts of our countryside have become green monocultures. Occasionally we can still see what some people will remember as once common: poppies growing amongst crops, bluebells in hedgerows, orchids in meadows, and blankets of *Sphagnum* moss in bogs. Draining, peat cutting, the increased use of chemicals and fertilisers, and overgrazing have led to much of the colour disappearing from our countryside.

Although Plantlife could be tempted to look back, yearning for the days before intensive agriculture, we do not. The future need not be bleak. Since Plantlife was founded in 1989 we have developed the *Back from the Brink* programme to rescue 99 endangered native plant species. Many of these species have consequently flourished and not one has since become extinct. Additionally, Plantlife's 4,000 acres of nature reserves protect threatened habitats and their rich diversity of flora. We have also raised awareness of the importance of wild plants to a whole new audience.

It is with growing influence and levels of achievement that Plantlife continues its work, knowing that we can halt the damage to our native flora of the past 50 years.

Flowers at my Feet stands as a record to the beautiful, wild places still to be found here. When you look at this book, and when you next go out into the countryside, you will appreciate the intricate, landscape-enhancing beauty of our native flora. But to ignore the health and wellbeing of our wild plants is not simply to deny our aesthetic pleasure. It is to threaten the very future of humankind.

ST. JAMES'S PALACE

This wonderful book provides the most vivid evidence that the British and Irish countryside is still home to an exquisite variety of wild flowers. It is remarkable that so much of our heritage of wild plants still survives. But with so many changes taking place the countryside faces an increasingly precarious future. Preserving wild species in our great botanical gardens, or in seed banks, is an important last resort, but no substitute for their wild and natural existence as an integral part of the countryside. To achieve this, every effort must be made to conserve their natural habitat and this must be our long term goal.

These photographs provide a splendid record of some of our most precious and beautiful natural habitats. They are an inspiration to us all to go out and explore the splendour of our countryside, and at the same time to think hard about what we need to do to ensure that our children and grandchildren can enjoy such sights for themselves. It would be a total tragedy if this book ever became a record of 'how things used to be'. That is the challenge Plantlife is taking up on our behalf and I believe they deserve every possible support in their task.

ACKNOWLEGEMENTS
Dave Woodfall

For myself both the process of working and the process of actually making a photograph is a meditation. This process can take a couple of years from initial pre-visualisation of an idea or a specific image I have in mind, or it can take a couple of minutes. That is why photography is such an exciting medium to work with. I have found that for me, this apparently random process only works when I am centered on myself, and the place I happen to be. It is the same whether I happen to be in Merthyr Tydfil or Venezuela, it's just that you get bitten by different things. For this reason I work best when I am alone or with a few people who are able to let me be myself.

My specific interest is how we interact with the world on which we live and how it interacts with us. I have an internal debate which ebbs and flows about this relationship. My photography is the end product of that debate. Perhaps all our relationships with the world consist of this debate, but for most it is an unconscious one, whether it is about survival or how many cars we can afford to own. It is my hope that this debate becomes a more public and open process, which doesn't only focus on short term priorities.

The landscape of Britain and Ireland and the conditions in which it allows our plants to develop into communities in turn, interact with other forms of wildlife and ourselves. Both Bob and myself hope that the contents of this book will create a greater debate in all of you. Only when this debate focuses into a co-ordinated all-party political policy for rural and urban landuse, and in particular for our wildlife communities, will our work be finished. It is only the closeness of wildlife experiences to all of our communities which will enable future generations to remain sane in an increasingly competitive world. This natural regeneration throughout involvement in the natural world whether it is for education, recreation or developing a business is key to our development as people.

However, none of the processes, which I outlined earlier would have worked in this book without the co-operation of the following people. Firstly for Bob for sharing his idea with me and allowing me to develop it within the project. For specific help I'd like to thank the following people for help in making these photographs. Mr and Mrs Bacon and the Suffolk Wildlife Trust, Malcolm Barton MBE, British Waterways, Mike and Sulwen Cambray, Les Colley, Val Corbett, Peter Corkhill, Corporation of London, Keith Cunningham, Fred Dreiling, Pete Fordham, Bob & Judy Foster-Smith, Ken Hoy MBE, Glynn Jones, Charlotte Lippmann, Richard and Joanne Moles, Pat and Angus MacDonald, Geoff Morries, David Painter, Jeff and Ruth Redgrave, Rick Southwood and Will Woodhouse from Bure Marshes NNR, Eilish Rothney and Anne and Rod Pattison. Everyone at Plantlife and HarperCollins*Publishers* who have helped enormously. I'd particularly like to thank Pat Tatton for her guidance.

Most of all I'd like to dedicate the book to my daughter Tesni Woodfall, whose sharp eyes spotted the Common Lizard close to the Wall Pennywort (pp.60–61). With love.

ACKNOWLEGEMENTS
Bob Gibbons

So many people and organisations have helped to realise this book, by responding to our advance notice in *Plantlife* magazine, replying to our enquiries, phoning up to tell us of impressive sights they have just seen, showing us around reserves and so on. Amongst those who I would particularly like to thank are: My partner Chris for support, help and ideas; Dr. John Akeroyd, Tony Bates, Andrew Branson, Martin Buckland, Clive Chatters, Ken Clarke, Kevin and Denny Cook, Tony and Bridget Davidson, the Bursar of Magdalen College Oxford, Brian Edwards, Ro Fitzgerald, Lorne Gill, Katherine Hearn, Tim and Barbara Hooker, John and Irene Palmer, Dr. Derek Ratcliffe, John and Val Roberts, Mike Scott, Julie Stobbs, Paul Toynton, Jean Wall, Robin and Jennifer Walls, and staff from the RSPB, English Nature, The National Trust, (especially their staff on The Lizard, Cornwall), The National Trust for Scotland, and many of the Plantlife staff especially Joe Costley, Joe Sutton, Nick Weiss and Jane Smart. Thanks also to the staff at HarperCollins for their professional and helpful approach, especially Katie Piper and Debbie Sellman. With apologies to anyone else who I have forgotten!

The photographs were virtually all taken on medium format Fuji film, usually Velvia for wider views and Provia for close-ups. Most were taken on a Mamiya 645 which produces 6 x 4.5 cm slides, but a few were taken with the extremely large and heavy Fuji GX 680 which produces larger pictures and allows lens movements to produce greater depth of field. The equipment is not critically important – the main requirement was to find top quality sites when they were at their best, and trying to photograph them in the most suitable or interesting light. Sometimes this proved straightforward when everything came together at once, but other sites had to be visited several times before a suitable photograph resulted. Foot and mouth affected the work considerably, as it took place during our main season of work; most of the effects were adverse, though it did produce some of the best displays of flowers for years where stock were temporarily removed. There were, of course, also many sites which were visited and photographed, but which have not appeared in the book because they were not quite good enough.

The whole process gave me a greater appreciation of the British and Irish countryside, and all who work to conserve it. Long may it continue. If we have helped to raise awareness and appreciation of our wonderful flora, then we have achieved our original aim.

SOUTH WEST

The Dodman Point with its magnificent views to Looe island in the east and the Lizard in the west lies at the heart of my favourite place. It is not the sea views, which are grand, across the treacherous waters off the point out across the Gerrans Bay, Gull Rock and on to Falmouth. Seething even when the rest of the ocean is dead calm. Nor is it the superb beaches at Hemmick and Vault which lie to either side of it. Indeed the Secret Beach at Hemmick only reachable at low water springs is fabulous. Here for a moment one can plan Robinson Crusoe discovering Man Friday's footprints in the virgin sand and climb the rocks to find caves once used by miners looking for copper. The verdigris-stained shales mark a moment long gone when the hewing of the earth made livings here, replaced now by those with leisure and curiosity to kill the time.

To a Dutchman like me, Dodman, a colloquialism of 'Doodman', meaning 'deadman', has the ring of dread to it. The cross, a marker for those at sea for more than a century, a reminder of mortality, its copper lightning conductor a marker for a more heavenly assault. There is a savage beauty here which has the capacity to either attract or repel, there are no half measures. It is not nice or pleasant and the stunted hawthorns and sheath of bracken speak not of hospitality, but survival against the elements. Yet, as you walk back along the coast path as if to go to Hemmick you come upon a sunken lane that cuts across the headland east to west. Lowering above you is a huge earthen bank with a smaller bank on the other side. These are the ramparts which once kept safe an iron age community who lived here two thousand years ago, their flints and metal work occasionally surface under the caress of the plough in the neighbouring fields.

Now you are walking in the ditch sheltered from the wind and in the spring the banks are rich with wild flowers; Herb Robert, Rosebay Willow-herb, Purple Loosestrife, Celandine, Campion both Red and White and Toad Flax are the stars. But the canvas is made of swathes of Wild Garlic, Alexanders and Cow Parsley. For a moment you are in a place of magic. Plates of time are overlaid here as each generation acted out their lives upon this stage. The human and the elemental merge in this passageway of sanctuary and you feel a sense of belonging to something that you can't quite put your finger on, but whatever it is, it feels good, like the rumour of Eden, just out of reach but … Tim Smit

Left Ox-eye Daisies, Common Sorrel, Quaking Grass, and other grasses, Lower Kingcombe, Dorset This picture was taken just before the sun set in the beautiful Dorset Wildlife Trust reserve at Lower Kingcombe. There is also a Burnet Moth pupa visible just below the right-hand Ox-eye Daisy – some indication of how valuable old meadows are for other forms of life. The Trust owns the whole farm, which it manages as an organic farm and nature reserve. (BG)

Mass of Sea Campion, Cornwall
Sea Campion is one of our most beautiful native plants, bursting into masses of flower in spring in the most exposed and difficult of coastal habitats, surviving gales and salt spray alike. This clump is growing on an old granite wall, covered with lichens, in west Cornwall, close to Cape Cornwall – perhaps the most oceanic part of mainland England. (BG)

Left
Kidney Vetch, Trevose Head, Cornwall
Kidney Vetch is always beautiful, but this mass of flowers on Trevose Head on the north Cornish coast was just stunning, photographed late in the evening. Coastal forms of this flower vary in colour from white to red, and most of the possible colour forms grow here together. The densest populations of flowers on this site were on old quarry waste. (BG)

Opposite

Clifftop Grasslands, Dinas Head, Cornwall
There is something particularly special about
the western British coasts, especially when
they are in full flower. The harsher and more
exposed the conditions, the denser the mass
of flowers is likely to be. The photograph shows
Thrift dominating the cliff-top grasslands,
looking out towards Dinas Head, on the north
Cornish coast. It is interesting to compare the
form of the Thrift seen here with that shown on
p.156, growing in a saltmarsh in the Outer
Hebrides at the opposite end of Britain, where
it is about one tenth of the height. (BG)

Left
Coastal displays, The Lizard, Cornwall
The displays of coast flowers around
Mullion Cove on The Lizard are amongst
the most spectacular to be seen anywhere.
The commoner coastal flowers such as
Sea Campion, Thrift and Kidney Vetch,
together with Primroses and Bluebells
(which thrive here as coast plants rather
than as woodland flowers) are all present in
wonderful abundance, enhanced by the
presence of many less common species
such as Hairy Greenweed. This scene, with
Primroses dominating, was photographed
soon after dawn, as the flowers catch the
first light. The site is owned and managed
by the National Trust. (BG)

Opposite

Sheep's Bit on sea cliff

The intense blue flower clusters of Sheep's Bit always come as something as a surprise, shining out from the grey lichen-covered coastal rocks. The more exposed the position, the better they seem to flower, thriving on the absence of competition. The main lichen here is Sea Ivory, abundant in the clean mild air of our western coasts. (BG)

Above left

Spring Squill amongst lichens and Stonecrop

Spring Squill flowers squeezing their way out between lichens and English Stonecrop leaves. This flower is often abundant, even dominant, on the unimproved grasslands of the western coasts of Britain, but almost absent inland and from the east coast. (BG)

Below left

Danish Scurvy Grass on an old wall, Cape Cornwall

Here Danish Scurvy-Grass is growing amongst lichen-covered granite boulders in an old wall, in the extreme west of Cornwall. Danish Scurvy-grass is most often seen as a tiny plant near the seashore (or nowadays along main roads, where the surplus salt allows it to survive), but here it grows luxuriously, totally in its element. (BG)

Below

Western Gorse and heathers, Dartmoor
For much of the year, the high moors of
Dartmoor appear to be almost flowerless; but
in late summer, Bell Heather, Ling and Western
Gorse all come into flower at the same time,
producing a fantastic carpet of purple and
gold, interspersed with clumps of the elegant
corn-coloured Bristle Bent. The photograph
shows Haytor, in the south-eastern part of the
National Park, in a brief sunny interval, with the
next Atlantic front rapidly approaching from the
west. Grazing by ponies, and other domestic
animals, keeps the moors in this condition.
(BG)

Flowers at my feet

Cornish Heath with Honeysuckle, The Lizard, Cornwall

Cornish Heath is a very rare plant in Britain, confined to just a small area of south Cornwall on the Lizard peninsula. Yet within this small region it is remarkably abundant, dominating large areas, and even forming hedges (of a sort) as shown here, with the red berries of Honeysuckle just projecting through its flowers. It varies in colour in the wild from almost white to deep pink, and, not surprisingly, it is widely cultivated in gardens. The best areas of Cornish Heath lie within The Lizard National Nature Reserve, or on National Trust land. (BG)

Below

Bell Heather, Ling and Purple moor grass, Dorset heath

The Dorset heaths are famous through the writings of Hardy, and also as a nature conservation issue since such large areas have been lost to agriculture and urbanisation in the last 200 years. Most of the best remaining examples are in south-east Dorset, especially on the beautiful Isle of Purbeck, where there are still areas large enough to support most of the special plants and animals. This fine example was photographed early in the morning on Hartland Moor National Nature Reserve, near Wareham. (BG)

Above
Lowland haymeadow, Kingcombe, Dorset
The ancient landscape of this part of west
Dorset still contains many places of significance
for nature conservation. The Dorset Wildlife Trust
and neighbouring Kingcombe Field Centre,
manage the farm to maximise both the biological
diversity and the understanding of visitors and
people attending the numerous courses there.
Many of England's lowland hay meadows are
but folk memories. The network of meadows at
Kingcombe all contain plants like Ox-eye Daisy,
Yellow Rattle, Meadow Thistle and Knapweed,
and are testament to what sensitive
management and co-operation can achieve.
(DW)

Above
Early Purple Orchids and Cowslips,
Hambledon Hill, Dorset
The prehistoric chalk hillforts of southern
England are often wonderful places for flowers,
mainly because they have rarely been ploughed
or used for intensive agriculture since prehistoric
times. The photograph shows the Iron Age hill
fort of Hambledon Hill (now a National Nature
Reserve) covered in Early Purple Orchids and
Cowslips, taken shortly after dawn in April. (BG)

Opposite

Corn Marigolds and Common Poppies, Dorset
Most cornfield weeds are a rare sight
nowadays, due largely to better seed-cleaning
methods and the use of herbicides. The seeds
are surprisingly persistent though, and it only
takes a slight change in management (such as
an absence of spraying) for the flowers to burst
into life. This field full of Corn Marigolds and
Common Poppies (together with many less
conspicuous weeds) was photographed near
Poole in July 2000; the following year, there
were virtually no flowers at all. (BG)

Below

Old lane bank and hedge, near Powerstock,
Dorset
This photograph represents both the purpose
and the conception of this book. I had been on
a Spring tour of southern Greece in 1999
where I had been eulogising about the masses
of roadside flowers. Shortly afterwards I visited
west Dorset which reminded me that the best
displays of flowers in Britain are as good as
almost anywhere in Europe. The photograph
shows an old lane bank and hedge near
Powerstock, alive with Wild Garlic, Red
Campion, Bluebells and much else, in late April
– a fantastic sight. (BG)

Flowers at my feet

Left

Flower meadow, Yeovil, Dorset

Ancient flowery meadows and pastures are such a rare sight nowadays that the impact when you do see a good one at its best is enormous. This beautiful field lies on the steep scarp slope just south of Yeovil in Somerset; in early May it is alive with Cowslips and Green-winged Orchids, to be followed later by a succession of other flowers. Once, most agricultural grasslands looked something like this, yet now only a tiny proportion remain, almost entirely managed as nature reserves since they are considered to have no place in modern agriculture. (BG)

Opposite

A closer view reveals the density of flowers in the meadow – Green-winged Orchids, Cowslips and Dandelion seed-heads, early on a misty spring morning. (BG)

Flowers at my feet

Previous pages
Devon hedgebanks in May
The older and shadier hedgebanks are often as rich in flowers as an old woodland (with many of the same species). The left-hand picture shows the uncurling fronds of Scaly Male Fern, growing with Greater Stitchwort and Bluebells near Dartmouth. In the right-hand picture, Wild Strawberry, Bugle, Germander Speedwell and Shining Cranesbill grow in close proximity on the shady side of a lane near Totnes in south Devon. (BG)

Left
Wild Snowdrops, Timberscombe, Devon
It is still not quite certain whether snowdrops are native in Britain or not. If they are, then this lovely valley near Timberscombe, on the north-eastern edge of Exmoor, is as good a candidate as any. The valley is filled with snowdrops in old woodland and pastures over a distance of about a mile, with few signs of past habitation or cultivation. It is a fantastic sight in February, though in the past few years it has become something of a victim of its own beauty and popularity. (BG)

Below
Roadside verge, Coney's Castle, Dorset
This beautiful wide roadside verge lies alongside a minor road across a hill called Coney's Castle in west Dorset, owned by the National Trust. Where roadside verges are shady and undisturbed, they act almost like woodland clearings, dominated here by Bluebells, Greater Stitchwort, Red Campion, and ferns such as Male Fern. This density of perennial flowers can only really be attained in ancient habitats. (BG)

Flowers at my feet

Left
Yellow Flag Iris, Somerset levels
The rhynes which bisect this lowland grazing marsh within an RSPB nature reserve, contain extensive stands of Yellow Flag Iris. The meadows in-between are significant for breeding waders with the hay crop being cut late to allow the young birds to fledge. During the winter these meadows are allowed to flood, attracting several species of wildfowl. (DW)

Left
Long-leaved Sundew, Dorset
Scattered through the Dorset heaths, there are many bogs, fed by unpolluted acid water from the surrounding heaths. These are home to a small band of specialised plants, many of which have developed an insectivorous habitat, to supplement their low intake of nutrients from their impoverished surroundings. One of the most frequent is the Long-leaved or Intermediate Sundew, shown here growing in an acid bog pool amongst *Sphagnum* moss. (BG)

Left
Dodder in flower, Exmoor, Devon
Wherever Western Gorse and heathers are abundant, it is likely that you will find the curious pink threads of Dodder, shown here with its tiny clusters of pinkish flowers in August. It is a total parasite, able to produce no food of its own, and since it is an annual, it needs to find a host each year. When it does well, as it is here on the Exmoor coast, it is a rather striking plant in its own right. (BG)

Above
Bullocks among Cowslips on Hod Hill, Dorset
I had come to the hill one early morning in late April after some friends had told me how good the Cowslips were. I hadn't intended to photograph the bullocks, but it soon became obvious what an integral part of the management they were (and anyway, they wouldn't leave me alone!). Hod Hill is crowned by an ancient and complex hill fort, dating back to Neolithic times with many later changes, and its ancient flowery chalk grassland is now managed as a National Nature Reserve, grazed with cattle through the summer, and sheep in winter. (BG)

Scarlet Elf-cup, Exmoor, Devon
Scarlet Elf-cup is a striking and rather unexpected fungus that appears in woodlands in south-western Britain from late autumn through the winter. It is shown growing here amongst Common Tamarisk Moss (though attached to dead wood underneath) on a frosty morning in February in a wooded Exmoor combe. (BG)

SOUTH EAST

How lucky we are in Britain to have such proximity to the natural world and the wild flowers and trees that contribute so much to it. The South East contains so many of the country's greatest wild open spaces.

My interest in the outdoors. I went away to school as a young boy. Presumably in the rather forlorn hope that it would keep us away from more adventurous pursuits, each of us was allocated a square yard of mud and issued with a packet of Virginia Stock seeds. Almost overnight I had my own square yard of vibrant colour. I was eight. I wanted to find out what was beyond the school grounds.

I treasure three things: conservation, diversity and choice. Much of our countryside is protected from building development, although the cost of that is eternal vigilance. Drive along the roads and urban sprawl overwhelms you. Fly by helicopter – *de rigueur* for a Minister of Aerospace – and the grounds for optimism are more evident.

Diversity is built into our system with the multiplicity of ownership and practice that exists. From roadside verges to the New Forest we have a treasure trove of abundance. And the combination that we have today, of massive public support and a dedicated conservation movement, offers the prospect of hope for the wild plants of Britain. **Rt Hon. Lord Heseltine**

Left Giant Horsetails, Hang Boy Slade, Epping Forest Epping Forest to the north east of London provides the largest area of native Beech woodland in the United Kingdom. These Giant Horsetails are growing in 'Tippa Bum' bog in Hang Boy Slade, one of a number of bogs which criss-cross the ancient woodland. Giant Horsetail is a relative of the giant ferns which helped form our coal measures many millions of years ago. The forest is managed by the Corporation of London who have restored the traditional management of this woodland once again. (DW)

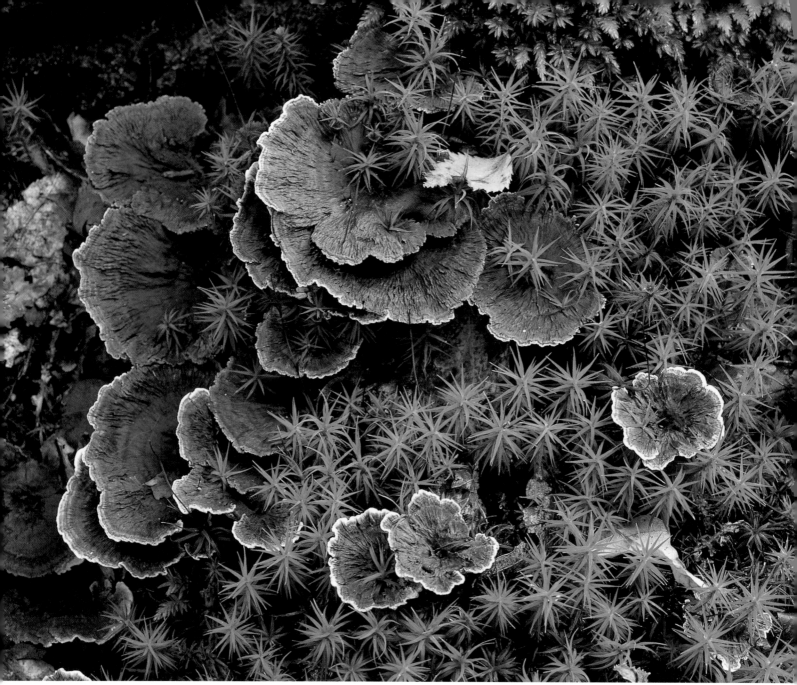

Above

Hydnellum concrescens growing in Hair Moss, New Forest, Hampshire

The tooth fungi (so-called because they have teeth instead of gills) include a number of rare species, and they are the subjects of many biodiversity action plans to conserve them. This unusual one, *Hydnellum concrescens*, one of Plantlife's *Back from the Brink* species, was growing on a wood-bank in the New Forest, amongst hair moss. The New Forest has one of the richest fungus floras of anywhere in Britain. (BG)

Above
Nottingham Catchfly
The striking flowers of Nottingham Catchfly,
which is not very aptly named since it has no
special association with Nottingham, and
doesn't catch flies, though some small insects
may become attached to the sticky hairs on
the stem. It grows mainly in dry calcareous
areas, and is often a good indicator of a
species-rich habitat. (BG)

Flowers at my feet

Previous page above left
Bell Heather and Wood Sage, Lullington Heath, East Sussex
There is a curious habitat that occurs here and there in southern Britain, known as chalk heath, where normally acid-loving plants such as heather grow abundantly on chalk downland, due mainly to a thin layer of acidic soil on top of the chalk. The resulting heath is always slightly different to normal heathland, and often has chalk-loving plants coming up amongst the heather bushes. Probably the best-known example of chalk heath is here at Lullington Heath near Eastbourne, now managed by English Nature as a National Nature Reserve. The picture shows Bell Heather And Wood Sage dominating the heath. (BG)

Previous page below left
Marjoram, Martin Down, Hampshire
A mass of Marjoram on chalk downland at Martin Down National Nature Reserve, Hampshire. Such masses of flowers are magnets for butterflies and other insects, yet this abundance of flowers is a difficult balance to achieve – too much sheep grazing, and the flowers are small and few, whilst too little grazing allows tall grasses and eventually shrubs to oust the finer herbs. The balance here is perfect. (BG)

Previous page above right
Marsh Mallow, Burham marshes, Kent
A wonderful display of Marsh Mallow at Burham marshes on the tidal section of the River Medway in Kent. The confectionery of the same name was originally prepared from extracts from the roots, though modern marshmallow sweets have no connection with the plant. It is a rather uncommon species in Britain, confined mainly to southern coastal areas; it grows particularly well on this Kent Wildlife Trust reserve, together with other rare plants such as Marsh Sow-thistle. (BG)

Previous page below right
Wild Chamomile, New Forest, Hampshire
Wild Chamomile was once quite a common plant over southern Britain, but its requirement for acidic heavily-grazed grassland, unimproved by fertilisers or herbicides, has caused its dramatic decline in the last half century, and it is now one of Plantlife's *Back from the Brink* species. One of its few last strongholds is the ancient lawns of the New Forest, grazed by ponies and cattle under a historic system of common rights, and untouched by modern agricultural chemicals. The photograph shows an exceptional display in the forest near Cadnam, photographed in early September. (BG)

Opposite
Marsh St. John's Wort
Marsh St. John's Wort is one of our most beautiful bog plants, its elegant sculptural shape, velvety leaves, and bright flowers lighting up the darkest peaty waters. This raft of flowers was floating on the surface of a black peaty pool, with water deeper than a fully extended tripod leg. It always comes as a surprise that such an exuberantly attractive plant should come from nothing but highly acidic nutrient-poor water and peat, but it does. (BG)

Left
Dandelions amongst Ground-ivy, on common land near Fordingbridge, Hampshire
Two of our commonest flowers, often described as weeds, yet they are as beautiful as many much rarer species. (BG)

Mass of Sea Kale, East Sussex

Any plant that can grow on seaside shingle, lashed by wind and salt and lacking any significant soil, has to be admired. Sea Kale is particularly striking, producing huge rosettes of fleshy leaves, covered with white flowers in early summer as if they were growing in the most fertile and sheltered of gardens. This superb display was photographed near Rye in East Sussex, on the excellent Rye Harbour Local Nature Reserve, better known for its bird life but home to some of the best shingle habitat in Britain. (BG)

Opposite

Great Sundew, New Forest, Hampshire

Only a few flowering plants manage to survive in really wet acid bogs, such as this one on Cranesmoor in the New Forest. Most of those that do are insectivorous, including the sundews, which have sticky hairs on the leaves to enmesh insects to be digested at leisure. The photograph shows Great Sundew, the largest and generally rarest of the three native sundews, which tends to grow in the wettest and most inaccessible parts of bogs. Although easily overlooked, they are remarkably beautiful in close-up. (BG)

Left

Bog Asphodels and Cross-leaved Heath, Ashdown Forest, East Sussex

These are two of our most widespread bog or wet heath flowers. Bog Asphodels are in the Lily family, and on close inspection, the flowers can be seen to be very similar to lilies. They do best where the habitat is grazed by cattle or other domestic animals, reducing the vigorous Purple Moor Grass, and allowing the flower spikes to show through. (BG)

Above

Pillwort, New Forest, Hampshire

Pillwort, one of Plantlife's *Back from the Brink*
species, along the margins of a lake near
Burley in the New Forest. In general, Pillwort (a
curious little grass-like fern that produces balls
of spores) is a rare and declining plant
throughout Europe, though where conditions
suit it, it can become abundant. The
combination of wet acid pond margin, and
heavy grazing and trampling by horses and
cattle here seems to favour its spread, though
it is threatened now by the invasion of New
Zealand Pigmyweed which tends to oust the
native plants wherever it occurs. (DW)

Above
River Water Crowfoot, **Rockbourne,
Hampshire**
Winterbournes are a fascinating feature of
chalk and limestone areas, rising and falling
according to the level of the underlying water
table. In the winter of 2000–2001 they were at
exceptionally high levels, thanks to the wettest
year on record. Because they are almost
exclusively spring-fed, they tend to be clear
and unpolluted, often supporting a rich and
varied flora and fauna. The photograph shows
the winterbourne covered with River Water
Crowfoot flowering profusely. (BG)

Flowers at my feet

Opposite
Heathland, Iping Common, West Sussex
A late summer evening on heathland in Sussex. The colours are entirely natural – a product of the last orange rays of the sun and the deep grey clouds of a clearing storm, though the effect only lasted for a few moments. Despite their natural appearance and special wildlife, most heaths are a product of man's intervention, occurring mainly where early man cleared forest over acid rock. Iping Common was one of the earliest such clearances, dating back to Neolithic times, and it is now managed as a Local Nature Reserve by the local council. (BG)

Above left
Purple Loosestrife and Common Fleabane, North Warnborough Green, Hampshire
These plants were photographed in flower in late summer at North Warnborough Green, in north-east Hampshire. The green is part of a fascinating series of commons associated with the River Whitewater that were once all grazed as part of the local agricultural system, though most are now neglected. The Hampshire Wildlife Trust manages this small common as a nature reserve, subtly maintaining its wonderful displays of flowers without allowing trees and shrubs to invade it. (BG)

Above right
Marsh Gentian, Bartley Heath, Hampshire
One of our most striking and exotic-looking plants, Marsh Gentian has beautiful large blue-violet trumpets. It grows best in wet heathland that is grazed or occasionally burnt, though often in such circumstances the plants tend to be dwarfed by the grazing effect. Here, at Bartley Heath in north Hampshire, they are both abundant and vigorous, producing beautiful plants with up to 20 large flowers. (BG)

Overleaf
Old Beech stump covered with fungi, New Forest, Hampshire
This photograph is intended to epitomise the Ancient and Ornamental woods of the New Forest. These are the ancient grazed woodlands, with huge scattered old trees but relatively little in the way of shrubs except for those that are tolerant of grazing and browsing, such as Holly. There is barely any ground flora, thanks to the heavy year-round grazing, but fungi, lichens, wood-boring insects, and hole-nesting birds all do well. It is an extraordinary survival of the medieval wood pasture, still large enough to be a fully working system. (BG)

Flowers at my feet

Spindle berries in Autumn
The berries of Spindle are one of the most striking sights of autumn, especially after a good summer when the colours are particularly rich, with their almost unreal combination of magenta and orange. (BG)

Flowers at my feet

Below
Frozen fen vegetation, East Stoke, Frome
Valley, Dorset
Although none of the plants here are in flower in
this February scene, they are still a visible and
important part of the view, contributing hugely
to our enjoyment of the countryside in any
season. The main plants here are sedges,
especially Lesser Pond Sedge, and Reed-
mace, with East Stoke Church just in view
across the old water meadows. (BG)

WALES

It's late July, 1971. The sun is flashing through the dense green foliage above the River Morlais; but the deep water is still freezing. We are three young boys enjoying life to its innocent limits. Our summer holidays have just started. A lifetime of school-free days lies ahead of us. Seven weeks, in fact. We are spending the whole day by the river; and in this more gentle age we swim, we rest on the flower-covered banks, we play some cricket. We are 9 years old. There isn't a parent in sight. It was like that then. Llangennech is a village in south-east Carmarthenshire; and what is now a disfigured, over-built urban sprawl was then a small village, hemmed in by sublime countryside and the glinting Llwchwr Estuary.

Trees. Glorious, gigantic, leafy trees. Hundreds of them. Wide, unruly gorse and bushes. Everywhere. And flowers. Wild flowers. Seemingly millions of them, carpeting every direction. These are the sparkling images of my youth; but they are as comfortingly vivid today as they were then.

My Wales is nothing without its landscape and country life. The natural industry of Wales is farming; and even the scarred industrial valleys have dumped their coal tips in favour of a more glorious terrain. In reclaiming land, these lovely valleys are also reclaiming their environmental heritage. It is a wonderful sight.

We now have a National Assembly devoting every working second to Wales. There can be few causes more important than the future of our countryside with its riches. We simply must conserve. Wild plants and flowers in their natural habitats are a glorious part of what we offer the world. So much has been lost; but so much can yet be secured. Huw Edwards

Left Coastal heath with Western Gorse and Bell Heather, Lleyn Peninsula and Bardsey Island, North Wales The extreme western slopes of the peninsula contain some of the best coastal heathlands in the British Isles. This has been achieved by careful and co-ordinated management of the coast through grazing by the National Trust, who own much of the coast of this area. The distinctive plant communities, which are all acid-loving plants, also contain nationally important numbers of Chough, which feed on the ants of these undisturbed grass and heath cliffs. (DW)

Above

Sheep's Bit, Pembrokeshire

Somehow, this wall could only be on the Atlantic seaboard of Britain, where the high rainfall allows plants to do well almost anywhere. This lovely old black stone wall is dominated by the blue of Sheep's Bit, together with Wall Pennywort, lichens, and other plants, photographed in Pembrokeshire in late May, near Abereiddy. (BG)

Right

Spring Squill among English Stonecrop, Pembrokeshire

The beautiful blue or bluish-purple flowers of Spring Squill, are a feature of coastal grasslands in western Britain, flowering profusely in early spring. This attractive group is surrounded, and enhanced, by the fleshy leaves of English Stonecrop, growing between lichen-covered rocks. Photographed in April on the Pembrokeshire coast near Strumble Head. (BG)

Below
Fungi with lichen and moss on tree stump,
Elan Valley, Powys
The lichen and fungi on a section of fallen Birch
tree in the Elan Valley, are indicative of the high
rainfall of over 60 in (1.5 m) a year. The upland
western Oakwoods are often characterised by
a less diverse ground flora compared to
wonderful shows of mosses, ferns and fungi
that are best seen from the autumn onwards.
(DW)

Following pages
Banded Snail eating Wall Pennywort,
Cerrigydrudion
This detail of a section of a low-lying west-
facing coastal hedge contains extremely
diverse floras from spring through to early
summer. This landscape often referred to as
'bocage' (of small fields, large hedges and
small woods) was depicted in Dylan Thomas's
Under Milk Wood and his poem *Fern Hill*. This
hedge bank was also playing host to a
Common Lizard enjoying the late April sun
between heavy showers. (DW)

Left

Sea Campion, Skomer National Nature Reserve, Pembrokeshire Coast National Park

These hummocks of Sea Campion cover many Puffin burrows which nest on this famous sea bird island. The naturalist Ronald Lockley made this and the nearby Skokholm Island well known through this passionate and lucid description of the natural world. It is managed by the West Wales Wildlife Trust and can be visited by boat and by arrangement one can stay on this beautiful island. (DW)

Opposite

River Water Crowfoot, River Wye, Powys

This section of the river, east of Builth Wells contains lovely water and grassland plants. The river is also flanked by a number of interesting Oakwoods. It was once one of the most famous Salmon rivers in the world. (DW)

Overleaf left

Common and Bell Heather on rock striated by glacier, Cwm Bychan, Snowdonia National Park.

The remarkable west-facing valley of Cwm Bychan inland from the town of Harlech contains a beautiful river, lake and Oakwoods. The slopes of the Rhinog mountains are carpeted with Common and Bell Heather as well as Cross-leaved Heath. Several thousand years ago the water beneath a glacier created this striations within the rock. Here a few clumps of heather cling to remaining clumps of peat. This valley had a profound influence on Robert Graves poem, *The White Goddess.* (DW)

Overleaf right

Reed Canary Grass, Tal y Llyn, Snowdonia National Park

Tal y Llyn a glacial lake at the southern foot of Cadair Idris is one of Wales most beautiful lakes; both Sea Trout and Salmon swim along this shallow river to the lake in order to breed. (DW)

Flowers at my feet

Opposite

Wood Anemones, Gwynedd

This small clump of flowers growing on a fallen stump of an alder tree is characteristic of the small woods and streams of eastern Gwynedd. The small and hard-pressed farms of this part of North Wales often leave marginal areas of small fields and woods which develop interesting floras.

Overleaf

Yellow Flag Iris alongside freshwater rhyne, Gwent Levels Site of Special Scientific Interest (SSSI)

The low-lying coastal freshwater marshes which lie between Cardiff and Magor in South East Wales are one of Wales unseen gems. Criss-crossed with rhynes and grazed with dairy and beef cattle it contains good hedgerows and meadows. The Countryside Council for Wales has worked hard with the farming community to maintain and develop the conservation value of the area in a sustainable way. Wentloog levels, one of the westerly areas of the Gwent levels, has been under sporadic threat of industrial development eating away at the margins of such peaceful and beautiful places. (DW)

Above

Early Marsh Orchid, Whitford National Nature Reserve, Gower

The calcareous dune slacks (damp hallows) contain high densities of several orchid species on one of the least disturbed sand dune systems in the United Kingdom. This small newly emerged flower is catching the last rays from the sun. The Countryside Council for Wales manages this National Nature Reserve with a sympathetic grazing requirement which has greatly increased the diversity of the flora over a period of several years. (DW)

Above

Cuckoo Pint or Lords and Ladies, Powys

This Oakwood with Hazel coppice is managed by the Radnorshire Wildlife Trust. It contains beautiful swards of Bluebells and large numbers of Early Purple Orchids as well as delicate plants such as this. (DW)

Flowers at my feet

Left
Cowslips in hedgerow, Denbighshire
These Cowslips growing in the shade of a
hedgerow oak tree in a farm lane in the Vale of
Clwyd are testament to the close relationship,
which exists between many farmers and the
natural world. The limestone of this part of
North Wales is particularly good for plants like
these cowslips. (DW)

Opposite
Primrose and Wood Anemone, Vale of Clwyd
A tiny fragment of native flora survives in a
corner of a highly modified wood. Many of
our small woodlands have been felled and
replanted with, in this case, beech trees.
The only clue to the fact that this is an ancient
semi-natural wood is the existence of native
Primrose and Anemones. (DW)

Above

Yellow Water Lilies, Bearded Lake,
Snowdonia National Park

Llyn Barfog, lying amongst hills in the south of
Snowdonia is a wonderful place to enjoy water
lilies. Much of this natural lake is covered in
Yellow Water Lilies, and a visit in late June and
early July will not be forgotten. (DW)

Flowers at my feet

Cowslips, Strumble Head, Pembrokeshire
A lovely group of Cowslips at Strumble Head,
Pembrokeshire, with the lighthouse beyond.
The coastal flowers of this part of west Wales
are quite exceptional, especially within the
Pembrokeshire Coast National Park. Cowslips
occur where the lime content of the underlying
rocks is slightly higher, such as here, and at
Stackpole, further south. (BG)

EAST ANGLIA

Harsh things are said about the landscapes of East Anglia, that they are flat, dreary and wind shorn, with no beauties of scarp or fell, no leaping streams or golden surf beaches, nothing to put in the brochure. What is the point of a walk if it doesn't unfold a constantly changing vista, give you a climb and a climactic panorama at the end? A better walk, to my mind, is the one that keeps you stopping all along the way because, as you cross bands of chalk, and rubble, and loam and sand, from wet to dry and back again, you encounter different plant colonies, unusual associations, new puzzles and new discoveries.

For the East Anglian walker it is not the glimpse of single rare species that is the principal pleasure, exciting though it may be, but seeing some of the commonest plants growing as they should, triumphing in their element. The same bell-bind that you struggle to extirpate in your garden, growing wild in chalk grassland becomes the spangled carpet on which the Scabious dance, Scabious that will change colour from dusky pink to blue as the soil conditions change. In East Anglia there grows a daisy for every day of the year, from the buttons of the spring, to the huge drifts of Ox-eye Daisies that reel up and over dry banks in early summer, and the Corncockle and Chamomile that will bloom as long as they can, even after the Wild Asters have announced the arrival of Michaelmas.

East Anglia is the brightest region of England, with more hours of sunshine than any other. Great shafts of light stalk over the fields; purple shadow masses chase each other up and down the banks. Every grass-blade is etched in light and even a spent seedcase can wear a halo.

Germaine Greer

Left Breckland, Wangford Warren SSSI, Suffolk Wangford Warren, a classic remnant of Sandy Breckland flora is managed as a Suffolk Wildlife Trust nature reserve. Before agriculture dominated much of East Anglia, the natural ground flora of acid-loving grasses and *Cladonia impexa* lichens dominated, with Silver Birch studded across this expansive landscape. Only a number of intensively managed nature reserves by both Suffolk and Norfolk Wildlife Trusts maintain those landscapes. Stone Curlew breed in a number of such places. (DW)

Great Bindweed and Hairy Willowherb, Ludham Marshes National Nature Reserve, Norfolk

The Norfolk broads are famous for their traditional boats known as 'wherries', which are still made on the edge of the grazing marshes, criss-crossed with dykes. It is the margins of these that contain plants such as Bindweed and Willowherb. A good range of marshland birds, including notably Reed and Sedge Warblers, nest along the dykes in clumps of surviving Common Reed. (DW)

Right
Windmill in reedswamp, How Hill, Norfolk Broads

How Hill is one of the more significant areas to visit in Norfolk to help understand the complex land use and ecology of the Broads. While to many, windmills are pretty ornaments strung across marshy fields, they are in fact practical tools to maintain water levels and enable agriculture and marshland to exist in close proximity. Here the reeds are harvested and used as thatching material for homes, pubs and businesses throughout the United Kingdom. A guided visit to How Hill with a Broadland Authority warden, either to gain an insight into the dependence of the wildlife on the management of the area, or simply to fill your lungs with air, is a joy. (DW)

Flowers at my feet

Fritillary Meadow, Fram Lingham, Suffolk
Several hundred thousand flowers sprout from
the bulb of this native flower alongside a
lowland stream, which is managed to flood in
winter creating the conditions necessary for
these fragile flowers. The site is managed by
Suffolk Wildlife Trust with the active co-
operation of the farm owners, Mr and Mrs
Bacon, and funded by English Nature. It can be
visited by arrangement in late April and early
May to enjoy these plants. (DW)

Bell Heather and Wavy Hair Grass, Dunwich
Heath SSSI, Suffolk
This east-coast heathland has eroded steadily
during the last century to rising sea levels. The
acid conditions of crumbly boulder clay are
ideal for extensive swards of Wavy Hair Grass
and Bell Heather. (DW)

Below right
Sea Pea and Yellow Horned Poppy, Suffolk
The aptly-named Shingle Street is a small
hamlet lying at the southern end of one of the
largest and most undamaged coastal shingle
systems in Europe. The photograph shows
two of the most distinctive and characteristic
of shingle plants – Sea Pea dominating the
foreground, and Yellow Horned Poppy behind,
– and gives a glimpse of the huge extent of
shingle beyond. Only the most specialised of
plants can colonise this habitat while it is still
mobile. The site lies at the southern end of the
huge Orfordness-Havergate National Nature
Reserve. (BG)

Flowers at my feet

Above and Opposite
Farmland, Ringstead, Norfolk
Most East Anglian farmland consists of sterile
arable land, free of intrusive weeds apart from a
few hardy species. Here and there, though,
there are oases of colour such as on Courtyard
Farm, near Ringstead in Norfolk, which is
managed with a strong conservation bias. One
part of the farm is managed specifically for the
old cornfield weeds which have now largely
disappeared elsewhere. The left-hand picture
shows White Campion, Common Toadflax and
other flowers growing along the margin of the
field in a pesticide-free environment; the right-
hand picture shows the mass of weeds that
can grow in a crop if allowed to, including Corn
Marigold, Cornflower, poppies, mayweeds and
others, photographed early on a misty July
morning. The adjacent areas are grazed by
cattle. (BG)

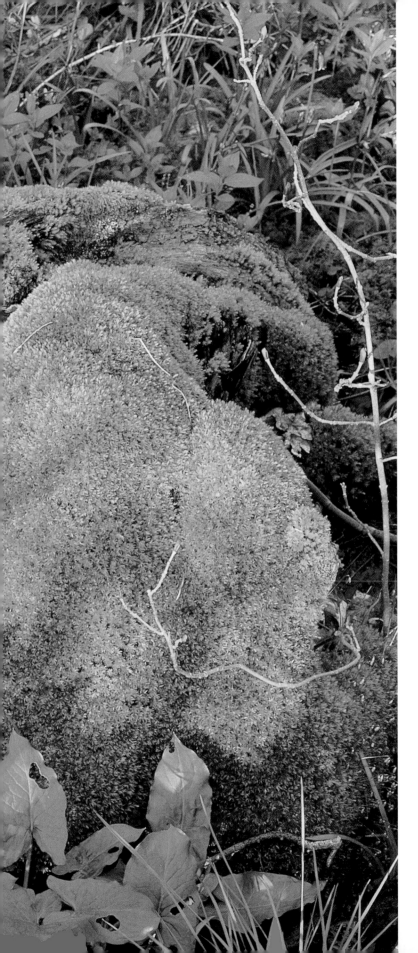

Stump of Ash tree covered in moss, Hayley
Wood, Cambridgeshire
Hayley Wood is one of the most highly
documented lowland woods in the United
Kingdom. Over a period of nearly 20 years
I've visited it numerous times and on this April
evening the wood was closer to a lowland
tropical rainforest with a foot of standing water
carpeting extensive areas. Unusually for an
east-of-England wood, Hayley is good for
mosses. (DW)

Opposite
Dog's Mercury and a rich variety of mosses on Ash tree bole, Hayley Wood, Cambridgeshire.
Dog's Mercury is one of the earliest woodland plants to emerge in the murk of winter. Enough soil has developed in the bole of this old ash tree to enable it to establish a precarious hold. Often our eyes are glued to the ground in the search for plants. Hayley Wood is a place which never fails to surprise me. (DW)

Above
Water-soldier, Bure Marshes, Norfolk
Bure Marshes National Nature Reserve contains wonderful examples of broadland birds, insects and plants. A Marsh Harrier quartered the reed beds and a late Swallowtail Butterfly thrilled me along one of the numerous rides on this early July morning. The extremely rare and native Water-soldier forms extensive mats on one of the dykes here. There is thought to be a direct link between the plant and the extremely local Norfolk Hawker dragonfly. (DW)

Above
Biting Stonecrop and Yellow Horned Poppy,
Snettisham, Norfolk
Biting Stonecrop flowering around a rosette of
Yellow Horned Poppy on stabilised shingle
near Snettisham, on the east coast of The
Wash. Yellow Horned Poppy is beautiful when
in flower (see p.81), but also has distinctive
sculptural non-flowering rosettes in its first
year of growth. (BG)

Left
Roadside Cowslips, Suffolk
The co-operation between the Department of Transport, County Councils and conservation organisations has ensured that a number of roadside verges retain interesting plants. This south-facing embankment, maintained partly by a reduction in roadside mowing, contains several thousand native Cowslips, which in turn attract early butterflies. (DW)

Following pages
Common Oak in ancient woodland with Bluebells, Garnett's Wood, Essex
This area of lowland Essex has a large number of extensive ancient woodlands dotted across intensively-managed agricultural landscapes. These woods are often linked by extremely wide hedges, which indicate the age of the landscapes and provide resting areas for a wide variety of birds, including Nightingale. (DW)

Marsh Marigold in managed Alder carr, Suffolk

The sound of the A14, which bisects this lowland Alder wood, betrayed the fact that it was not a remote rainforest. This local nature reserve, managed by the district council, contains a raised boardwalk and plants such as Marsh Marigold around this recently-coppiced Alder tree. The cut wood is used to make charcoal which can be smelt on summer evenings from barbecues in the nearby town of Stowmarket. (DW)

Flowers at my feet

Above
Bugle and ancient Small-leaved Lime, Garnett's Wood, Essex
Many of these trees are hundreds of years old, and their rotational cultivating has allowed enough light to penetrate to the woodland floor, enabling these and nearby clumps of Early Purple Orchids to establish themselves. This ancient woodland is now managed as a Local Nature Reserve in Essex and, although not well known, is a real link between the present and the past in this fascinating part of Essex, north west of Chelmsford. (DW)

Above
Bladderwort, Ludham Marshes National Nature Reserve, Norfolk
It is only when you are immersed in the same place as these fragile plants that the wonder of their existence is experienced. They contain small 'bladders' to trap insects which are then ingested as food. (DW)

Above left

Marsh Pea, Bure Marshes NNR, Norfolk

A reed gently shaken by wind holds the delicate tendrils of this rare plant. For me this plant symbolises the fragility of our native flora and is testament to the hard work of the staff and volunteers of Bure Marshes, where this simple photograph was taken. (DW)

Above right

Pasque Flowers, Barnack Hills and Hollows, Lincolnshire

Pasque Flowers are one of our most beautiful native flowers, as well as being amongst the rarest. They flower in April, round about Easter (hence the name *pasque*, from the French for Easter), pushing up through grass that is still brown to produce their exquisitely beautiful flowers. These were photographed at Barnack Hills and Hollows, a fascinating area of old limestone quarries near Stamford managed as a National Nature Reserve, and carefully grazed with sheep. (BG)

Left

Oxlip, Hayley Wood, Cambridgeshire

The colour of this plant is startling in its subtlety. Nothing can prepare you for it. Growing only in a small area where Bedfordshire, Cambridgeshire and Suffolk meet on damp boulder clay. Pack your wellies and look for a clearing in old woodland here in mid-April. (DW)

Left

Upper Saltmarsh, Norfolk

The North Norfolk coast has some of the most extensive and natural saltmarshes in the country, now mostly protected within nature reserves of some sort. In late summer, when the Sea Lavender flowers, they are a mass of colour as far as the eye can see. The photograph shows some upper saltmarsh near Burnham Overy Staithe with Common Sea Lavender, Sea Arrow-grass, Sea Purslane, and other specialist saltmarsh plants, photographed in late July. (BG)

Flowers at my feet

Left

Biting Stonecrop on an old tiled roof,
Ringstead village, Norfolk

This species of stonecrop, also aptly known as
Wall Pepper, occurs naturally on shingle and
rocks, but its tolerance of dry nutrient-poor
conditions has allowed it to colonise roofs and
walls, clothing them in bright yellow flowers
through the summer. It's not always easy for
householders to leave it growing on roofs, but
when they do, it looks marvellous. (BG)

Left

Wood Anemones amongst coppice lengths,
Bradfield Wood, Suffolk

The relationship between sustained woodland
management and increased ground flora
diversity has been well documented. However,
much of this woodland has been left to develop
into high forest, which is important for
invertebrate populations. The lengths of Alder
(seen here) and Hazel branches are cut into
spars, which are ideal for holding thatch in
place. This ancient woodland sustains a
number of traditional crafts, which are
important for both practical and educational
purposes and are a credit to the Suffolk Wildlife
Trust who manage the wood. (DW)

Flowers at my feet

Above
Yellow Loosestrife, Strumpshaw Fen, RSPB
Nature Reserve, Norfolk
Unlike many marshes it is possible to walk
round extensive areas of this beautiful reserve.
Although not a common plant, at Strumpshaw
Yellow Loosestrife does form extensive swards
in this valley fen. The meadows are good
places for small mammals and on the evening I
made this photograph a Barn Owl quartered
the marsh. (DW)

MIDLANDS

Meadows are the essence of the Midlands, land of hayfields and lazy rivers and the Lark. I was born in Northamptonshire and my happiest childhood memories were playing with the lambs – their woolly legs yellowed with Buttercup pollen, and the May hedgerows capped, so I thought, with ice cream.

The Midlands then were gold and silver and blue.
Like a skylit water stood
The Bluebells in the azured wood.

The Nene still meanders through rushy meadows around Oundle, and there the Lady's Smock survives, and the Orange Tip Butterflies which feed upon it, flap their wings like little torches, dipping over the pale mauve petals. Sometimes a Kingfisher sits below the Mill Bridge watching the bubbles around the Yellow Water Lilies. Long ago I was shown a Kingfisher's egg, and never forgot that sphere, as white as snow and as round as a golfball.

Somewhere in the Midlands' mini-cornbelt, someone dismayed and depressed by the deserts created by modern agriculture, left 75 acres of ploughed fields untouched by man, and undisturbed for 50 years. No more mammoth machines, no chemicals, no clouds of dust, no huge bales of hay, looking like dinosaurs' droppings in the fields. The assiduous Grey Squirrels, the Jays, the mice, the wind and the rain, and seeds dropped from the fur and faeces of passing foxes, have planted these fields with 224 species of flowering plant, grasses and ferns, bushes and trees, which include four species of wild roses – some climbing the trees – a sheet of hairy Violets, Cowslips, Forget-me nots, Bird's Foot Trefoil, a stand of Bee Orchid, a Crab Apple and 60 sturdy Oaks. Seventy species of bird have demonstrated their approval …

All you have to do is watch and marvel. Walk through the long grass starred with wild flowers and note the Goldfinches busy among the teasels. Decide to create a miniature nature reserve! Save our flora. The Midlands have shown us the way. Dame Miriam Rothschild

Left Haymeadow, Withybrook This beautiful organic haymeadow, dominated by Cat's Ear and Meadow Buttercup, is part of Elmshurst Organic Farm in Withybrook, east of Coventry. Mr and Mrs Pattison manage the farm with a beef herd, and sell produce in their farm shop. Careful stewardship of this farm, including a wide range of wildlife habitats which have been created there, is good evidence of the link between the quality of our landscape and the quality of food produced. The Countryside Agency has a project currently in operation called 'Eat the View', to draw attention in all regions of England, to such beneficial land management practices.

Above

Pyramidal Orchid, Lady's Bedstraw and Bird's-
foot Trefoil, Cranham Common,
Gloucestershire

The summer of 2001 found this extensive
Cotswold common with much denser grasses
and large numbers of Pyramidal Orchids. The
south- and west-facing slopes were barely
grazed because of the threat of foot-and-mouth
disease. As a result, butterfly, grasshopper and
cricket populations increased significantly. (DW)

Above

Unimproved grassland, Clattinger Farm

At the right time of year, the meadows of
Clattinger Farm hit you like a wall of colour.
The farm consists of over 60 hectares of
grassland in the floodplain of a tributary of the
Thames on the Wiltshire-Gloucestershire
border. Most of the farm has not been
agriculturally improved in the modern sense,
and the density and abundance of flowers is
quite extraordinary. The photograph shows
one of the larger fields, dominated by a rayed
form of Common Knapweed, Meadowsweet
and Yellow Rattle, with Common Spotted-
orchid and Hairy Hawk-bit amongst others.
The whole farm is now owned and managed
by the Wiltshire Wildlife Trust. (BG)

Left

Old Oak in Buttercup field, Warwickshire
Common Oak is the archetypal British tree, and
a meadow full of Buttercups is often thought
of as a typical piece of countryside, yet both
are becoming harder to find. This old Oak,
damaged by lightning but recovered, was in a
flowery pasture near Henley in Warwickshire.
(BG)

King-cups at Cricklade, Wiltshire

North Meadow, on the Thames floodplain near Cricklade in Wiltshire is best known for its extraordinary displays of Snake's-head Fritillaries in April, but it also has a remarkably diverse flora of many other species. During the years 2000 and 2001, it flooded particularly strongly during winter and late into the spring, and the fritillaries failed to do well. By contrast the King-cups, which can cope better with standing water, had a very good season. The whole huge meadow is managed as a National Nature Reserve, retaining its ancient management of winter flooding, summer hay cut, and aftermath grazing. (BG)

Reed-mace, Market Bosworth, Leicestershire

The Reed-mace lining extensive sections of this Midlands canal is an indication of the greater priority British Waterways is giving to the conservation of native flora in the 21st Century. Long stretches of this canal, which snakes through beautiful Leicestershire countryside, contain interesting and developing communities of plants. Because of this, the Ashby Canal has been declared a Site of Special Scientific Interest. (DW)

Above
Greater Stitchwort and Goldilocks,
Buckinghamshire
Greater Stitchwort and Goldilocks flowering
profusely along the edge of a Chiltern wood
in Buckinghamshire. The white Stitchwort is
common enough in a variety of habitats, but
the Goldilocks, with its curiously-deformed
petals, is one of the better indicators of an
ancient woodland or hedgerow, failing to
survive long once the trees are removed.
(BG)

Above

Wild Pear, Worcestershire

The fallen fruits and leaves of Wild Pear in a
Worcestershire meadow near Hanbury. The
true Wild Pear is a spiny tree with fruits that are
almost spherical rather than pear-shaped, and
are hard and inedible. There is some doubt as
to whether the Wild Pear is a true native tree,
though there are records of it in Anglo-Saxon
boundary descriptions, so it has certainly been
here for some while. (BG)

Flowers at my feet

Poppies, near Painswick, Gloucestershire
This poppy field, the result of a combination of reduced chemical sprays and disturbance from ploughing catches the last rays of summer. The valley, immediately north of Stroud, was under threat from development, until local people and the CPRE campaigned successfully for the area to remain undisturbed. (DW)

Flowers at my feet

Left

Snake's-Head Fritillaries, Oxford

Snake's-head Fritillaries were once quite
common in the floodplains of central England,
but are now confined to just a few meadows
in conservation ownership, due to increased
drainage, floodplain housing development, and
general agricultural improvement. The meadow
shown here is one of the most extraordinary, a
mass of fritillaries in April, yet it lies in the middle
of Oxford just behind Magdalen College. The
college treasure and protect the meadow,
which is as historic as any of the city's buildings.
(BG)

Following page left

Flowers in a ploughed area, Salisbury Plain

Amongst the vast tracts of chalk downland that
make up the Salisbury Plain Military Training
area, there are little patches that are ploughed
to provide seed and cover for game birds.
Often these areas produce a riot of colour in
June, as seeds of 'weeds' buried in the soil
suddenly find conditions to their liking. This
patch contains a dense mass of Nodding
Thistle, White Campion, and Viper's Bugloss,
superb for butterflies as well as birds. (BG)

Following page right

Wild Daffodil, Bettyhill Wood, Gloucestershire

Oak standards with Hazel coppice and a
wonderful show of Wild Daffodils at one of the
Gloucestershire Wildlife Trust nature reserves.
In the 19th Century, large numbers of visitors
travelled by train to see such displays and now
these sites increasingly provide important
places for people to enjoy wildlife and
understand our role in maintaining a varied
and interesting landscape. (DW)

Left

Common and Sharp-flowered Rush, Seaton Meadows, Rutland

Flowery old meadows and pastures are at a premium in the midlands, where intensive agriculture has converted most of them to grassy monocultures or arable fields. Those that have survived are usually nature reserves, such as this Plantlife reserve at Seaton Meadows in Rutland. The photograph shows Common and Sharp-flowered Rush in one of the wetter areas, though it is probably better known for its Great Burnet, Ox-eye Daisy and other more colourful species. (BG)

Opposite

Wild Water-cress, Wiltshire

Wild Water-cress in a small chalk stream close to its source near Calne, in Wiltshire. Water-cress particularly favours the warm nutrient-rich waters of chalk streams, where it often grows in company with the rather similar Fool's Water-cress (which is poisonous!). (DW)

Left

Downland, Avebury, Wiltshire

Avebury rings and stone circle, in Wiltshire, is an exceptional archaeological and historical site of international importance. However, like many ancient sites, it also has a rich flora thanks to the long history of grazing without ploughing or chemical applications. This photograph shows the abundant late summer downland flora on the outer ramparts, consisting mainly of Burnet-saxifrage, Small Scabious, and (out of the picture) the rare Tuberous Thistle in its hybrid form. In 2001, the flowers were particularly good, as the sheep had been removed due to the foot-and-mouth outbreak (though they would soon go if it was not grazed at all). (BG)

Opposite

Wild Angelica and Meadowsweet, Cauldron Canal, Stoke-on-Trent

North of Stoke-on-Trent runs is one of Britain's most beautiful canals. British Waterways have decreased their moving regimes on ecologically sensitive sites, and Wild Angelica, Valerian and Meadowsweet drift along the edge of this quiet canal. (DW)

Left

Mistletoe growing on an old apple tree in Herefordshire, near the Welsh border

Although by no means a rare plant, Mistletoe always seems special, and is the subject of many legends. The Herefordshire and Worcestershire apple-growing area is one of its main strongholds, where it is encouraged as an additional cash crop, and there are mistletoe markets before Christmas in Tenbury Wells. (BG)

Flowers at my feet

Left

Autumn hedgerow near Silverstone, Northamptonshire

The old enclosure hedges of this area, dating from about 300 years ago, are rich in trees and shrubs, especially on the limestone or the more lime-rich clays. In autumn, they are at their best as the fruits of Elderberry and Bramble (both shown here), together with Crab Apple, Hawthorn, Rowan, and other species ripen in the sun. (BG)

Opposite

Wild Garlic, Greenwood Trust Nature Reserve, Ironbridge

Less than half a mile from the birth of the Industrial Revolution this woodland is testament to the regenerative power of the natural world. The industry of this famous valley utilised the woods for charcoal, and now the Greenwood Trust run courses in traditional crafts utilising wood in everything from coracle-making to swirl baskets. The scent of this Wild Garlic wood now is very different from the smells emanating from this valley 300 years ago. (DW)

NORTH

From the flanks of great Dun Fell where the icy fingers of the last glaciation still make Gentians and Globe Flowers feel at home, east to Holy Island where Yellow-wort finds its northern limit, and west to the warm wet coastline of the English lakes, the north still puts on its annual show of wild flowers.

All this despite the fact that it is has been people-managed for at least 5,000 years. Polished stone won from quarries on the Langdale Pikes allowed Neolithic farmers to destroy the ancient forest, opening windows of opportunity for the diverse flora of pastures and haymeadows ablaze with colour. While coppice woodlands provided a continuity of sylvan cover and their own special mix of light and shade, some with sheets of bluebells. Lime-rich bedrock and drift still work their magic, clints and grykes in the wetter west and unique mixes of plants almost at sea level on the magnesium limestones.

England's largest National Nature Reserve and the world's second most-visited National Park sit astride the Pennine ridge. Now covered with blanket mire, a multicoloured living tapestry of the bog mosses bejeweled with Cranberry, Bog Asphodel and Bog Cotton, one of the rarest types of vegetation in the world, all set about with heather moor where bees make honey and grouse and sheep may safely graze.

Past mismanagement has also played a crucial role. Quarries, gravel workings and spoil heaps provide conditions too harsh to support lowland weeds so giving space in which Grass of Parnassus and Bird's Foot Trefoil can do their thing. While Meadow Cranesbill and Sweet Cicely crowd the verges of winding lanes and motorways alike on which Sainfoin finds its northern limit.

All this and so much more is now being nursed back into working order by what I like to call the green renaissance. Partnerships of caring people, in which Plantlife champions the flora in all its glory. **David Bellamy**

Left Cranberry in flower, Cumbria The delicate flowers of Cranberry, looking like miniature cyclamen, pushing up through a mass of *Cladonia* lichen on a bog in north Cumbria. (BG)

Left

Meadow Crane's-bill and Meadowsweet, Teesdale, Co. Durham

The traditional haymeadows of Teesdale are known throughout the world. Their management by landowners and tenants produces the sweetest hay. The wildflower meadows' biological richness is maintained by active co-operation between English Nature and the farmers and landowners of this beautiful dale. The characteristic plants of northern haymeadows, Meadow Cranesbill and Meadowsweet, are growing here in a damp corner of a meadow alongside a drystone wall. (DW)

Above

Limestone flora, Thrislington, Co. Durham

A band of Magnesian limestone runs across north-east England, but the flowery grassland that once covered much of it is now reduced to a few fragments. It differs from most limestones in its high magnesium content, which influences the flora that grows there. This shows the best remaining fragment, at Thrislington Plantation National Nature Reserve, with Bird's-foot Trefoil, Spotted and Marsh Orchids, Tufted Vetch, and the endemic English subspecies of Perennial Flax. This beautiful area of grassland stops short on the edge of a large active quarry – a reminder of what could easily have happened to the rest of the grassland in the absence of protection. (BG)

Opposite

Grass of Parnassus, Ainesdale National Nature Reserve

Stretching from the Ribble Marshes in the north, to Liverpool in the South, the Merseyside coast has been a huge conservation success story. Grass of Parnassus flowers in August through to mid-September, and particularly well in the damp, dune slacks of Ainesdale National Nature Reserve. Staff and volunteers from a wide variety of conservation organisations have worked tirelessly to improve the natural history interest of the coast. They provide evening guided walks to listen to Natterjack Toads that call in these same sand-dune slacks, on April evenings. (DW)

Flowers at my feet

Below and Opposite
Grazed and ungrazed grassland, Peak District

The deeply-incised limestone valleys of the southern Peak District – the White Peak area – are superb places for flowers. The slopes are usually too steep for ploughing or fertiliser application, so they have been traditionally grazed with sheep or cattle, allowing a wide range of flowers to flourish. The left-hand picture shows grazed grassland at Monsaldale on the River Wye, dominated by Common Rock-rose; the right-hand picture shows ungrazed grassland dominated by Bloody Crane's-bill in Deepdale, just east of Buxton (not the Deep Dale recently purchased by Plantlife). Several other similar valleys are protected as nature reserves. (BG)

Flowers at my feet

Opposite top
Hay Meadow flora with Wood Crane's-bill and
Pignut, Swaledale
Farmers have managed the meadows for hay
since the time of the Vikings and here, at
Muker, it is possible to walk through them
on a public footpath. The North Pennines
Environmentally Sensitive Area Agreement has,
to some extent, made it easier for farmers to
conserve such areas. (DW)

Opposite below
Rosebay Willowherb, Lindisfarne,
Northumberland
Although we tend to think of Rosebay
Willowherb as a plant of waste ground or old
bomb-sites (hence its alternative name of
Fireweed), it is also common in more natural
sites. This fabulous mass of flowers was on the
sand-dunes at Lindisfarne (Holy Island) in
Northumberland, in the National Nature
Reserve. (BG)

Left
Dyer's Greenweed, Co. Durham
When I first walked this coast over 20 years ago
there were still pit heads on the beach and the
effects of heavy industry dominated and the sea
was black. Now plants like Dyer's Greenweed,
normally found in undisturbed haymeadows, are
colonising this raised beach immediately south
of Seaham in County Durham. (DW)

Marsh Marigold, Leighton Moss, Lancashire
While making this photograph, a Bittern boomed
in the nearby reedbeds. During World War I
potatoes were grown here, but with many of the
estate workers leaving to fight, the drains
became blocked and the area reverted to marsh
and swamp. Since the 1960s, the RSPB has
managed the site to create extensive reedbeds,
Alder and Willow carr. Many thousands of
people enjoy the experience of visiting the hides
and boardwalks of Leighton Moss. (DW)

Left

North Lancaster Canal, Tewitfield, Lancashire
The margins of Lancaster canal are, in certain
places, of exceptional botanical interest. British
Waterways has actively developed this through
selective mowing and allowing the margins to
develop along the canalside footpath. So
visitors on a July evening are as intoxicated
equally by the smell of drifts of Meadowsweet,
as they are by the carbon dioxide from the
immediately adjacent M6. Modern Britain in
microcosm. (DW)

Above

Roadside verge, Pennines

A beautiful flowery roadside verge high in the
Pennines near Alston, with Lady's Mantle,
Wood Cranesbill, Water Avens and other
flowers growing in profusion. Although there
are flowery meadows left in this area, the
roadsides are often the best places to see
meadow flowers, since they are unploughed
and unfertilised and normally not grazed too
heavily. (BG)

Above

**Heather growing through Juniper,
Swinesdale, Lake District National Park**

The remote valley of Swinesdale contains
extensive Juniper bushes, one of Plantlife's
Back from the Brink species, amidst block
scree, which has tumbled down from the side
of this U-shaped valley. A number of valleys in
the Lake District, particularly where the density
of grazing sheep is not too great, have
established Juniper woodlands, which have
distinctive invertebrate populations. (DW)

Flowers at my feet

Right

Emerging Common Reed, Leighton Moss, Lancashire

These reeds are symbolic of the future of this marsh. They provide nesting cover for warblers, Bearded Reedling, Bitterns and Marsh Harriers, as well as a place for Otters to hunt for eels. This area within the marsh has received intensive management to remove old reed, through selective burning, and in a few years will be a thriving reed bed once again.

If left to itself, in a few years the reeds would dry out and prevent the valley from becoming colonised by Willows and Alders. The RSPB has created a variety of habitats that suit the needs of a large diversity of wildlife. (DW)

Left

Water Lobelia, Blea Tarn, Lake District National Park

Restricted to the glacial lakes of western upland, Britain, this graceful plant grows in the margins of these lakes with only tentative foothold amidst the gravel and stones. Dragonflies often use these plants to rest on while hunting insects. (DW)

Following pages

Alston Wood with a carpet of Bluebells, Lancashire

Dawn light touches a Sycamore and Ash tree in this wood, which runs along the River Ribble. One of a series of woods in this valley containing plants like Toothwort, Yellow Star-of-Bethlehem and Yellow Archangel, it is one of the loveliest places that I know. These are the Bluebells that make our woodlands the envy of botanists throughout Europe. (DW)

Flowers at my feet

Left

Species-rich haymeadow, Pen-y-Gent, Yorkshire Dales National Park

Where old meadows do still exist in the Yorkshire Dales, they are wonderful places, full of flowers and insects, and often with abundant nesting birds. This beautiful grassland is on the slopes of Pen-y-Gent, photographed early on a June morning. The main flowers visible are Pignut, Red Clover, and both Meadow and Bulbous Buttercups. (BG)

Common Rock-rose and Bloody Cranesbill on limestone pavement, North Yorkshire
Wherever the glaciated carboniferous limestones outcrop in Yorkshire and Cumbria, they tend to form the aptly-named limestone pavements. A scoured roughly level surface is seamed with deep shaded solution cracks known as grykes, and the resulting combination supports a curious mixture of plants with affinities to limestone grassland, mountain rock ledges, and shady woodland. The photograph shows Scar Close National Nature Reserve in North Yorkshire, with Common Rock-rose and Bloody Cranesbill in the foreground. (BG)

Flowers at my feet

Above
**Flower-rich meadows with Wood Cranesbill,
Pignut and Sorrel, Swaledale, Yorkshire Dales
National Park**
Swaledale contains some of the most
significant upland hay meadows in the United
Kingdom. They are testament to the consistent
management carried out by the farming
community in what is for me one of England's
most beautiful valleys. (DW)

SCOTLAND

Flowers have always inspired poets. And Scotland's flowers always make me think of poetry – especially the exalted poetry of Hugh MacDiarmid in his *Lucky Poet* (1943):

Scotland small? Our multiform, our infinite Scotland small?

Only as a patch of hillside may be a cliché corner

To a fool who cries 'Nothing but heather!' where in September another

Sitting there and resting and gazing around

Sees not only the heather but blaeberries

With bright green leaves and leaves already turned scarlet,

Hiding ripe blue berries; and amongst the sage-green leaves

Of the bog-myrtle the golden flowers of tormentil shining …

'Nothing but heather!' – How marvellously descriptive! And incomplete!

I think of the Bluebells of Scotland. I think of drifts of nodding Bluebells carpeting our ancient woodlands (properly speaking Harebells – and even more properly speaking, Wild Hyacinths). I think of the other delightful plants which nestle on our woodland floors: One-flowered Wintergreen, Twinflower, Small Cow-wheat. I think of the extraordinary floral fecundity of the *machair* meadowlands of the west-coast mainland and the Outer Hebrides, the result of centuries of traditional crafting husbandry. I think of the beautiful and unique pink Scots Primrose (*Primula scotica*), now confined to a few bastions of exposed clifftop turf in Orkney, Caithness and Sutherland. I think of the natural rock-gardens of our high wildlands, with their Alpine Mountain Avens, Alpine Gentian, Alpine Forget-me-not, Alpine Fleabane and Alpine Milk-vetch – many of them extremely rare, all of them exemplifying Hugh MacDiarmid's impassioned plea to look at Scotland's flowers with open eyes. There's Heather, of course, in all its forms, mantling the hills with a deep autumn purple and playing host to innumerable other delights: Blaeberry (Bilberry), Cranberry (Cowberry) and Bearberry. And in the marshlands and lochans we find Bogbean, Yellow Flag Iris and Marsh Violet … 'Nothing but Heather'? Don't you believe it! Magnus Magnusson KBE

Left Hair mosses among lichen-covered rocks, Glencoe A lovely mixture of upland lower plants growing on acidic rocks in Glencoe, west Scotland, where the average rainfall is very high. The main lichens visible are *Porpidia* and *Rhizocarpon* species on the rocks, with Hair Moss *Polytrichum* producing its delicate capsules in the spaces between the rocks. (BG)

Purple Oxytropis, Bettyhill

Purple Oxytropis growing on the convoluted, metamorphosed mica-schist rocks near Bettyhill on the north coast of Scotland. This is one of our rarer plants, confined to a few places in Scotland, though much more widespread on mountains in mainland Europe. Bettyhill is a well-known spot for its rich flora, thanks to its northerly latitude and great variety of habitats, many of which are now protected within a National Nature Reserve. (BG)

Above

Dwarf Willow, Caenlochan, Angus

High mountain vegetation on Caenlochan, on the south-eastern edge of the Cairngorm massif. The main plant is Dwarf Willow, a tiny relative of willow trees, that rarely grows above 8 cm (3in) high, and often much less. Plants at this altitude have to survive many months under snow, and frosts for most nights of the year, so it is hardly surprising that they are dwarf. (BG)

Right

Channelled Wrack and Spiral Wrack, Kylestrome

The sea-lochs of western Scotland have a fantastic diversity of marine life, including an abundance of seaweeds, thanks to their clean cool water, and relatively sheltered conditions. Terrestrial viewers can only see a fragment of the diversity when the tide recedes. The photograph shows Channelled Wrack and Spiral Wrack in a sea loch, at low tide, near Kylestrome in the far north-west of Scotland. (BG)

Flowers at my feet

Scottish rock plants

In areas of high rainfall, where long periods of summer drought are a rarity, rocks and stones become a relatively hospitable place to grow in, and many rare plants do well here, in the absence of too much competition. The photograph on the *left* shows Common Wild Thyme flourishing in a crack with Sea Ivory lichen on cliffs on the north coast. Most exposed areas of the rock are covered with other species of lichens. *Top right* shows English Stonecrop growing amongst flat pebbles just above high water mark near Stranraer, in south-west Scotland. *Bottom right* shows a clump of the extraordinarily beautiful Purple Saxifrage growing from a crack in mica-schist high on Ben Lawers in Perthshire. This is one of our hardiest plants, producing a mass of flowers at high altitudes in northern Britain as early as late March, just as the main snow mass begins to melt. (BG)

Right
Bell Heather amongst *Cladonia* lichens,
Dornoch Firth
A distinctive vegetation type on the coasts of
eastern Britain is the lichen heath. Large areas
of stabilised sand dunes or shingle become
dominated by a slow-growing sward of lichens,
especially *Cladonia* species, creating a strange
sight, like a rumpled grey blanket spread over
the landscape. This photograph was taken at
Dornoch Firth, in north-east Scotland, showing
Bell Heather pushing through the all-embracing
carpet of *Cladonias*. (See also p.166.) (BG)

Flow Country landscape

The extraordinary Flow Country of north-east Scotland is one of the most distinctive landscapes of Britain, dominated by huge areas of blanket bog, with natural pools, and occasional mountains. It has a quality of wildness that is hard to match anywhere else in Britain, and has a wonderful richness of breeding birds, plants and invertebrates. Its wilderness qualities have been threatened in recent years by extensive drainage and planting of conifers, leading conservation organisations, such as the RSPB and Plantlife, to purchase substantial areas for their protection. The photograph shows a dramatic midsummer view in the RSPB'S Forsinard reserve. (BG)

Left
Mountain flowers on ledges of Ben Lawers, Perthshire
Ben Lawers is one of Britain's most famous mountain flower areas, notable for its rarities and displays of common flowers alike. The ungrazed mica-schist ledges are alive with species such as Moss Campion, Rose-root, Purple Saxifrage (not in flower here) and Alpine Forget-me-not, amongst many others. The whole mountain is owned and managed by the National Trust for Scotland. (BG)

Opposite
Sphagnum moss and Common Sundew, Brora
A close-up of a bog surface on the southern edge of the Flow country, near Brora in Sutherland. The green and red bog mosses (two different species of *Sphagnum*) form the basis of the bog, growing on upwards whenever the water level rises. The rosettes of the insectivorous Common Sundew dot the surface, surviving in these inhospitable acid nutrient-poor conditions by catching insects and digesting them. (BG)

Flowers at my feet

Mass of Thrift on Saltmarsh, Carnish, Outer Hebrides

A fantastic display of Thrift, or Sea Pink, in upper saltmarsh near Carnish on the Hebridean island of North Uist, with the mountain of Eaval beyond. The fascinating pattern of channels, from which the sea drains back after most high tides, give an attractive structure to the marsh. It is worth comparing the size of these plants with those on the cliffs in Cornwall (see p.15). (BG)

Left

Munsary Peatlands, The Flow Country

The Plantlife nature reserve here contains several bog pools, or Dubh Lochs, characteristic of a tundra landscape. It is also important for breeding birds. However, an adjoining forestry plantation threatens the biological integrity of both flora and fauna. It is not just the management of nature reserves themselves which is important, but also the landscape of adjoining areas which can have dramatic effects on the interests of the natural world and its protection. (DW)

Below

Mossy Cyphel and Moss Campion, Perthshire

Mossy Cyphel is a little-known plant confined to mountains (and occasionally lower altitudes) in the northern part of Scotland. It produces a gradually-enlarging hummock, with a woody base, and it is probable that the largest hummocks such as this one are very old. Here, the old hummock is ringed by, and has partially engulfed, clumps of Moss Campion in the Breadalbane Mountains, Perthshire. (BG)

Opposite

Mass of flowers by falls on the Dochart River at Killin, Perthshire

The flowers seen here are an intriguing mixture of grassland plants, weeds and introduced species – Ground Elder, buttercups and the North American Monkey-flower, of which several species are now widespread along our rivers. (BG)

Flowers at my feet

Below

Field of Spignel, Glenshee, Angus

A field full of the strangely-named Spignel, or Baldmoney, near Glenshee in Angus. This is a widespread mountain plant of central and northern Europe, which occurs sparingly in hilly areas in Britain between central Scotland and north Wales. Spignel only survives where there has been little agricultural improvement, and this field has escaped intensification thanks to its small size and proximity to a village hall. (BG)

Masses of Clustered Bellflower and others on sand dunes, Fife

A fantastic display of high summer flowers on the stabilised sand dunes at St. Cyrus National Nature Reserve, north of Montrose. Clustered Bellflower is more abundant here than almost anywhere else in Britain, growing with Rosebay Willow-herb, Common Restharrow, Hogweed, Ragwort, Lady's Bedstraw, Marram Grass and much else of interest. (BG)

Left

Machair, South Uist, Outer Hebrides

Machair is a Gaelic word now widely used to describe the open flowery habitats that develop on blown calcareous shell sand on the most exposed Atlantic fringes of Britain. The sand blows in to mix with the existing soil, forming a fertile, calcareous and well-drained substrate; such areas may be simply used for extensive grazing, or they may be cultivated from time to time, then allowed to revert to rough pasture, producing a wide range of different *machairs*. The photograph shows a close view of an area recently used for Barley, but now covered with Wild Pansy, Common Storksbill, Field Forget-me-not, White Clover and other common but attractive flowers. (BG)

Previous page left
Grassland, Loch Insh, Spey Valley
A fascinating area of flowery grassland near
Loch Insh in the Spey Valley, within the RSPB's
Insh Marshes reserve. The grassland is
dominated by an unusual combination of
flowers, including Northern and Lady's
Bedstraws, Zig-zag Clover, Harebell,
Sneezewort, Common Knapweed, Lady's
Mantles and Eyebrights. There is a wonderful
mixture of habitats in this area, rich in all forms
of natural life. (BG)

Previous page right
Monkey-flower and Creeping Forget-me-not,
Glen Devon, Perthshire
Although Monkey-flower is an introduced
species, originally from western North America,
it has become a characteristic – and very
attractive – part of our riverside vegetation in
many areas. Here it is growing in apparent
harmony with a mass of the native Creeping
Forget-me-not by the river in Glen Devon in
Perthshire. (BG)

Opposite
Machair on the south-western coast of South
Uist, Outer Hebrides
This beautifully flowery coastal grassland
(see pp.162–163) is dominated by Bird's-foot
Trefoil, Silverweed, Lady's Bedstraw,
buttercups, daisies and other flowers – all
common species, but occurring here in
fantastic density producing an extraordinary
tapestry of colour. The continuation of
displays such as this depends heavily on the
continuation of a traditional low-intensity way
of farming. (BG)

Above
Lichens and Bell Heather, Dornoch Firth
Cladonia lichen heath, with Bell Heather, on
stabilised sand and shingle by the Dornoch
Firth in north-eastern Scotland, extending
away as far as the eye can see. (See also
pp.150–151.) (BG)

IRELAND

SACRAMENTS OF COLOUR AMONG THE STONES

by John O'Donohue

The Burren is a kingdom of limestone sculptures carved slowly by rain, wind and time. Everywhere light conspires to invest these stone shapes with ever changing presence. Limestone is a living stone. Perhaps because it holds and returns echo so clearly, I have felt since childhood that there might be a secret music locked within the limestone here. Though it amazed strangers, it never seemed strange to us that these limestone fields could entice the most exquisite wildflowers to emerge here.

As the grip of winter loosened, the landscape gradually returned from bleakness graced with subtle sacraments of colour that always made the stone seem kind. Profusions of Gentian surfaced like blue stars from the clay. White and purple Orchids rose higher to offer their quiet grandeur to wider view. Mountain Avens softened the stonescape with their gentle white and yellow countenances. And in crowds Harebells crept up towards the breeze from the ocean. For millennia the farmers here have been he secret keepers of these fields. They know their names and contours. After winter they know where to go looking for the new arrivals. We need to recognize and encourage the care the farmers give. More faithful than tourist or scientist, they are the native priests and priestesses of the Burren. John O'Donohue

John O'Donohue is the author of the international bestsellers *Anam Cara: A Book of Celtic Wisdom* and *Eternal Echoes: Exploring our Hunger to Belong*, and his latest book is a collection of poetry, *Conamara Blues*.

Left Grassland *Machair*, **Doagh Island Nature Reserve, Donegal** On the southern shore of Trawbega Bay, near Mallin town, is a special example of coastal *Machair*. Here, dwarf examples of Bird's Foot Trefoil and Bulbous Buttercups carpet the gently undulating sand hills. Grazed by cattle from the local community, *Machair* is also important for Corncrake and Chough. This bay has been under the shadow of aquaculture development for several years, despite it being an important site for its marine fauna. (DW)

Yellow Flag Iris, Connemara
Nowhere are Yellow Flag Irises more abundant than in the rough marshy grazed fields of south-western Ireland. The photograph shows a wonderfully flowery wet pasture, edged with stone walls in Connemara, with the Twelve Bens and a departing storm in the distance. (BG)

Above
Mountain Avens on limestone, The Burren
Only a few yards from the high watermark of the coast, near Black Head, this arctic alpine plant finds an unlikely place to grow amidst the limestone pavement of the Burren. Mountain Avens is one of several plants which characterises the arctic alpine flora of the Burren, made possible by the Atlantic Gulf Stream. (DW)

Lichens, Clifden, Connemara
Coastal rocks at Aillebrock, near Clifden on the west coast of Ireland. These rocks, in the mild unpolluted air, are home to a fantastic display of lichens, covering virtually every square inch of the rocks. Species here include Sea Ivory, Tar Lichen, Orange Sea Lichen and Common Orange Lichen amongst others, occupying different zones according to their tolerance of sea water or spray. Seawards, they grade into a dense band of marine algae ('seaweeds'), whilst the higher parts are colonised by Thrift, Bird's Foot Trefoil and other flowers. (BG)

Left
Bloody Cranesbill growing in limestone pavement, Gryke Burren
The limestone pavement surrounding Loch Gaelin contains some of the most significant flowers of the Burren. Known as Mullagh Moor, the area adjacent to the site managed by *An Taisce* (National Trust for Ireland) was to be developed for a visitor centre, until plans were overturned. The development would have had a serious impact on the biological integrity of one of Ireland's most significant sites for nature conservation. Containing Dwarf Hazel woodland, a tourlough, limestone pavement and grassland, it never fails to make my heart beat faster. (DW)

Left
Wall Pennywort on al old wall, Beara Peninsula
Wall Pennywort, or Navelwort, growing in serried ranks from the cracks of an old wall on the Beara Peninsula, south-west Eire. In the mildest western counties, this plant can grow almost anywhere. (BG)

Flowers at my feet

Left

Sea Milkwort on shingle, Killarney, Co. Kerry

Sea Milkwort growing amongst rocks on the upper shore of an inlet near Killarney. This beautiful little flower grows in highly saline areas such as saltmarsh and stony beaches all round the coasts of Britain, though its best displays tend to be in the north and west. It is actually much more closely related to primroses than milkworts. (BG)

Opposite above

Mass of lichens on old wood

Part of a wonderful collection of lichens growing on an old fence post in the far west of Ireland. The species include the red 'match-sticks' of *Cladonia floerkeana*, greyish-green beard lichens, at least two species of *Parmelia*, and the common *Hypogymnia physodes* (visible at bottom right and bottom left). (BG)

Opposite below

Heath Bedstraw, Dunmanus Peninsula, Co. Cork

Heath Bedstraw growing on metamorphic rock on the Dunmanus Peninsula in County Cork, south-west Eire. This little plant forms large mats, covered with flowers – easily missed, or stepped on, but very attractive on closer inspection. (BG)

Below

Pond Water-crowfoot, Bandon River,
Co. Cork

The Bandon River in County Cork, south-west
Eire, brimful of flowering water crowfoot in
June. This species – Pond Water Crowfoot –
normally grows in stiller waters, but this river
is slow enough, and unpolluted enough, to
allow it to flourish. Sights such as this soon
disappear if the river is affected by industrial
or agricultural pollution. (BG)

Below

White and Yellow Water-lilies, Co. Donegal

Western Ireland, and especially the higher
rainfall areas of the north-west, is dotted with
dark peaty freshwater lakes. These vary widely
in their flowers, but many are covered by White
Water lilies. This particular one, in County
Donegal, has both White and Yellow Water-
lilies, photographed on a windy, stormy
summer's evening. (BG)

Coastal grassland, The Burren, Co. Clare

The Burren, in County Clare and County Galway, is one of the most fascinating landscapes in Europe, and one of the best botanical sites in the British Isles. The rocky limestone grasslands are intensely flowery, with many rare or unexpected flowers. The photograph shows beautifully flowery coastal grassland, including typical limestone outcrops, with Burnet Rose, Bloody Cranesbill, hawkbits, Common Rock-rose and other flowers, to the south of Ballyvaghan. (BG)

Hare's Tail Cottongrass, Blanket Bog, Co. Kerry

Looking towards Ballydavid Bay and Mount Brandon beyond, this hill top bristles with Horsetail Cotton Grass. The Dingle peninsula is the most westerly land in Europe and Eire's current prosperity has seen a growth of communities which had become bereft of people towards the end of the 19th Century. The nature conservation of this part of Eire depends on their involvement in regenerating the environment which should make the economy more sustainable. (BG)

Above
Coastal and rock plants, Giant's Causeway,
Co. Antrim

The Giant's Causeway, in County Antrim, is one
of the most distinctive landscapes anywhere,
still beautiful despite its tens of thousands
of visitors each year. In the less-trampled parts,
the hexagonal basalt columns support an
attractive mixture of coastal and rock plants,
including Thrift, Wild Thyme, Bird's Foot Trefoil,
and lichens. The whole area is a World Heritage
Site and Area of Special Scientific Interest,
owned and carefully looked after by the National
Trust. (BG)

Above
Low tide with seaweeds, Roundstone Bay,
Co. Galway
The cool, clear, unpolluted waters of the
Atlantic coast of Ireland are incredibly rich in
seaweeds, both in terms of biomass and
species diversity, as well as in the animals that
depend on them. This view across
Roundstone Bay, at low tide, reveals the extent
of the seaweed beds to be found in the more
sheltered areas, away from the pounding of the
open ocean. (BG)

Churchyard with wildflowers, Kilcatherine,
Beara Peninsula, Co. Cork
On the Beara Peninsula there is a lovely old
ruined church at Kilcatherine, romantically
situated close to the west-facing coast. The old
churchyard remains, full of wild flowers such as
Sheep's Bit, Cat's Ear, Thrift and an abundance
of grasses, constantly buffeted by the westerly
winds – the climate of this part of the world has
been described as 'a series of westerly gales
interspersed with periods of strong winds
and rain'! (DW)

AFTERWORD

Our aim throughout this book has been to try to show some of the finest displays of flowers and other plants to be found in Britain, and to show just how impressive these displays still are. They compare well with the best to be found anywhere in Europe. That they exist at all is a tribute to the dedicated staff of organisations such as English Nature, the Countryside Council for Wales, Scottish Natural Heritage, the National Trust and all the county Wildlife Trusts, to name but a few. Although these sites are essentially natural (though admittedly usually modified in some way by man), it requires considerable skill and knowledge to keep them in a suitable condition for the plants and animals that occur there, and it requires time, money and persistence to protect them from the changes going on all around them. Both of us knew Britain pretty well before embarking on this project, but it would be fair to say that we both found many new places – as well as old favourites – that took our breath away.

The other side of the coin, however, is the increasingly obvious fact that one has to

Above
Lack of natural vegetation, Walsall
How many of us are able to retain an interest in, or a memory of wildflowers and their importance to us, while we shop in places which are increasingly removed from the natural world? The reality is however, that many of our urban areas contain many places which are important for wildflowers, and should be equally cared for as are more rural locations for flowers. (DW)

travel long distances between these top quality sites, often through countryside almost bereft of wildlife, or through heavily built-up areas lacking in any real high quality wildlife. The figures for the decline of our habitats are all too well-known, though it's worth repeating just a few here – about 97 per cent of our flowery meadows have become single-species monocultures since 1945, and in the same period, 96 per cent of our peat bogs have been drained, and 78 per cent of open heaths lost in one way or another – a sad catalogue of losses. This inevitably increases the pressure on the remaining sites, not only in terms of visitor numbers, but also in their significance as the best remaining examples of once-widespread beautiful, fragile, semi-natural habitats.

People's response to such negative change varies. Rod and Anne Pattison's response to such negative and widespread change has been to produce an ecologically sustainable farm ten miles to the east of Coventry. Elmsworthy Organic Farm (see pp.100–101) contains stunning hay meadows and a variety of wildlife habitats including restored hedges, ponds and many thousands of newly planted trees. These support a beef suckler herd, the meat of which is marketed by their own farm shop, which supplies a wide range of organic food throughout the region. Registered as a soil association farm for a number of years it is testament to how a business can satisfy the demands of the market place in addition to maintaining and improving the wildlife interest of a farm, which adds of the value of the farm products.

Grace Wheeldon, who lives close to Millers Dale in Derbyshire, has been involved with the Derbyshire Naturalists and then Wildlife Trust since 1965. Her involvement led to the Trust purchasing Priestcliff Lees, which eventually led to Millers Dale being declared a National Nature Reserve. She was encouraged to record the flora of the area by the then conservation officer, Pat Brassley in the early 1980s and through both recording and management work has increased the numbers of Dark Red Helleborine, Early Purple Orchids and Cowslips. More recently she has been involved at Plantlife's

Above
Destruction of Offham Down
In 1997 this downland SSSI was ploughed to be re-seeded with flax, thanks to legislation which allowed European Community grants to be used to destroy important wildlife sites. As a result of the farmer's actions, there was a massive upwelling of feeling from people in Sussex, who reinstated the turf. These areas have responded well with the majority of the wildlife interest intact. Currently, unless a farmer has had an Environmental Impact Assessment carried out on a site, it is not possible to plough unimproved grassland. (DW)

reserve at Deepdale with biological recording. She initially and continues to be involved because of the realisation that no one else was going to do it, so it had to be her. Deepdale is her favourite place and feels that her involvement shows what an individual can do to ensure that we all have flowers at our feet.

Flowers at my feet

DON'T LET BRITAIN'S COUNTRYSIDE LOSE ITS COLOUR

Britain's countryside is in danger. In danger of losing the wild flowers that give it its unique local variety and its colour. Many counties have already lost up to a quarter of their native wild plants. In some regions, a species is lost every year. By letting these distinctive wild plants decline to the point of extinction, we risk destroying the habitats of butterflies and other insects, birds, reptiles and mammals, creating a countryside that is dull and devoid of local character and colour. Will you become a member of Plantlife today?

We stand on the brink of a major natural disaster and we must act urgently. So please take positive action yourself – join Plantlife now. Professor David Bellamy OBE, President, Plantlife

PLANTLIFE

Yes, I'd like to save our wild plants and their habitats

Mr/Mrs/Miss/Ms/Title _____

Name: _____

Address: _____

_____

_____

             Postcode: _____

Choose your own subscription level

Members tell us that they are happy to choose their own level of annual membership subscription, so we set no fixed amount. We ask you to choose the amount you prefer to pay from the range of options below. Each subscription provides the same membership benefits.

£24 would pay the expenses of supervising volunteers on a day's wild flower rescue work.

Here is my preferred membership subscription of:

☐ **£16** ☐ **£20** ☐ **£24** ☐ **£50** ☐ **£100**

☐ **£400** **Life membership**

Gift Aid

___/___/___
(please date)
I want Plantlife – *The Wild-Plant Conservation Charity* to treat as Gift Aid all donations, subscriptions and gifts I make, until I notify you otherwise.

___/___/___
(please date)
I am NOT a UK taxpayer, and regret that I cannot participate. (Remember that if you receive a company pension, income tax may well be paid at source, and you would therefore qualify.)

I enclose my cheque/CAF cheque payable to Plantlife

OR

Please debit my MasterCard/Visa/Switch*/CAF CharityCard

for £_____

Card number:

☐☐☐☐ ☐☐☐☐ ☐☐☐☐ ☐☐☐☐ /

☐☐☐ * If using a Switch card, please use the long number from the middle of your card.

Start date: .... Expiry date: ....

Switch issue no: ....

Signature:..

☐ I am not quite ready to become a member yet.

Please accept my donation of £_____

Data Protection Act. As a member you may like to receive information about the work of other reputable organisations. If you would prefer not to receive this information, please tick the box. ☐

Please return to:
Dr Jane Smart,
Executive Director,
FREEPOST LON 10717,
London SW1W 9YY.

PLANTLIFE

Patron: HRH The Prince of Wales
Plantlife – *The Wild-Plant Conservation Charity* is a charitable company limited by guarantee. Registered Charity No. 1059559 Registered Company No. 3166339 Registered in England.

Payment by Direct Debit - Instruction to your Bank or Building Society

Name and address of your Bank or Building Society

To: The Manager _____

Bank or Building Society _____

Address _____

_____

           Postcode _____

Name of Account Holder _____
As printed in your cheque book

Branch sort code ☐☐ ☐☐ ☐☐

Account No: ☐☐☐☐☐☐☐☐

Originator's identification number:

☐7☐ ☐2☐ ☐5☐ ☐4☐ ☐5☐ ☐6☐

Originator's reference:
(please leave blank)

Instruction to your Bank or Building Society.
Please pay *Plantlife - The Wild-Plant Conservation Charity* Direct Debits from the account detailed on this instruction subject to the safeguard assured by the Direct Debit Guarantee

Signature: _____

Date: _____

Bank and Building Societies may not accept Direct Debit Instructions for some types of Account

PLANTLIFE

The Publishers, Authors and Plantlife would like to thank all those who have contributed to this book.

Tim Smit is Chief Executive and co-founder of the Eden Project, near St Austell in Cornwall. Following his move to Cornwall in 1987, he and John Nelson discovered Heligan, the subject of a popular television series and book, *The Lost Gardens of Heligan*.

Michael Heseltine has enjoyed one of the most colourful and creative careers of modern British politics. A great supporter of the British countryside, he has a particular interest in trees, and has his own arboretum at his house in Oxfordshire.

Huw Edwards is presenter of the BBC's *Six O'Clock News*, the UK's most watched news programme. He combines his newsreading duties with a wide range of radio music broadcasts.

Germaine Greer has been a feminist icon since the 1960s, when her first book, *The Female Eunuch* took the establishment by storm, and has since written several other books. She is Professor of English and Comparative Studies at the University of Warwick.

Dame Miriam Rothschild is a world-renowned scientist and dedicated conservationist with a lifetime love of Lepidoptera. During her distinguished career she published over 300 scientific papers, but now concentrates on the conservation of British flora.

David Bellamy is one of Britain's best-known environmental campaigners. An international botanist, author and broadcaster, he holds a number of academic posts including Special Professor of Botany at the University of Nottingham.

Magnus Magnusson KBE, writer and broadcaster, was the founder-chairman of Scottish Natural Heritage (1992–97). He lives in the country, north of Glasgow.

John O'Donohue is the author of the international bestsellers *Anam Cara: A Book of Celtic Wisdom* and *Eternal Echoes: Exploring our Hunger to Belong*. His latest book, *Conamara Blues*, is a collection of poetry.